WHY ARE CHEMICALS NOT NAMED JOHN?

Naming Chemical Compounds 6th Grade Children's Chemistry Books

Speedy Publishing LLC

40 E. Main St. #1156

Newark, DE 19711

www.speedypublishing.com

Copyright © 2017

All Rights reserved. No part of this book may be reproduced or used in any way or form or by any means whether electronic or mechanical, this means that you cannot record or photocopy any material ideas or tips that are provided in this book

There over a hundred elements that make up the matter of our world and universe. They combine to make thousands and thousands of compounds. How do we keep them all straight? Here's how scientists name chemical compounds!

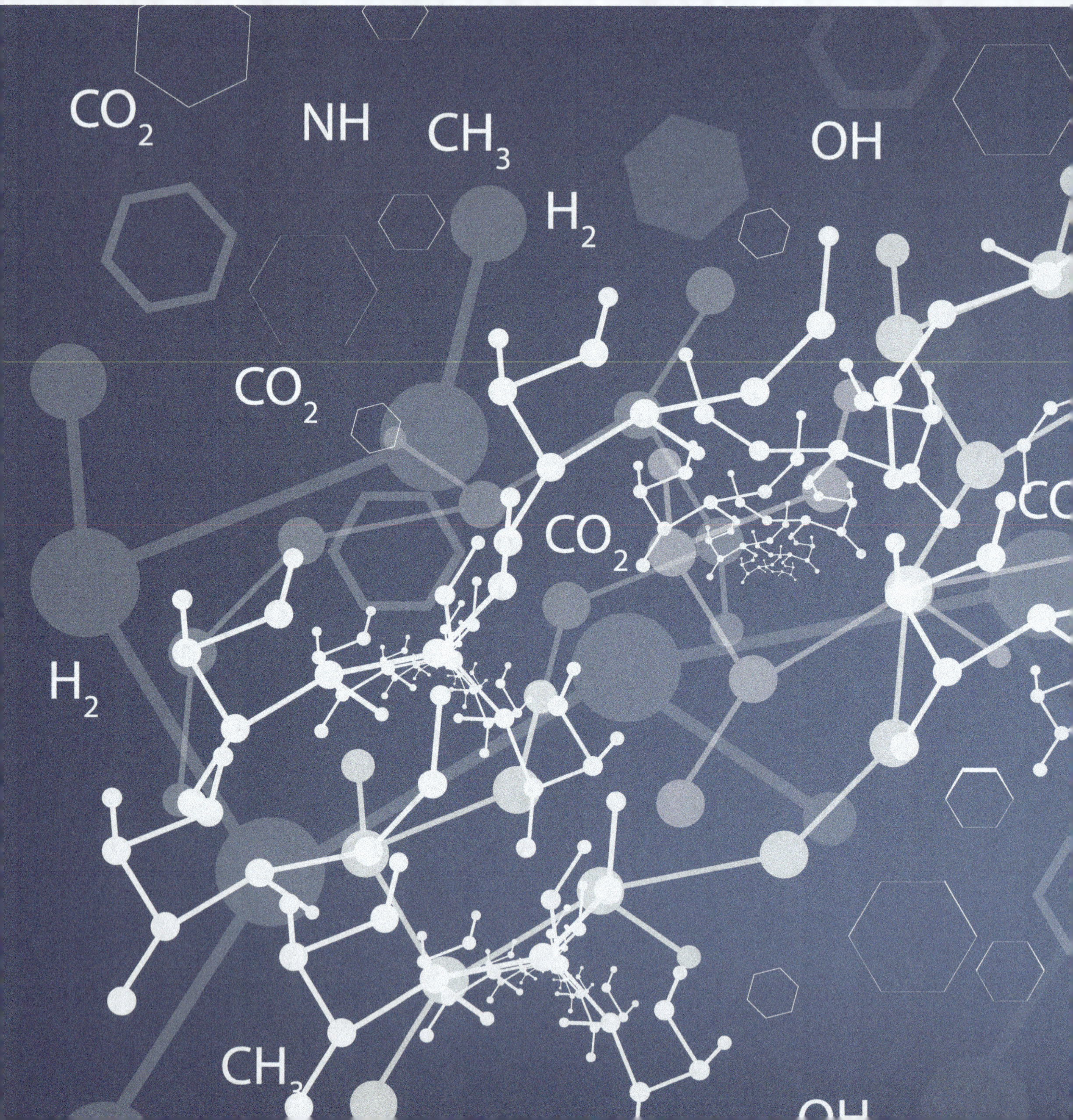

CO$_2$
NH
CH$_3$
OH
H$_2$
CO$_2$
CO$_2$
CO
H$_2$
CH$_3$
OH

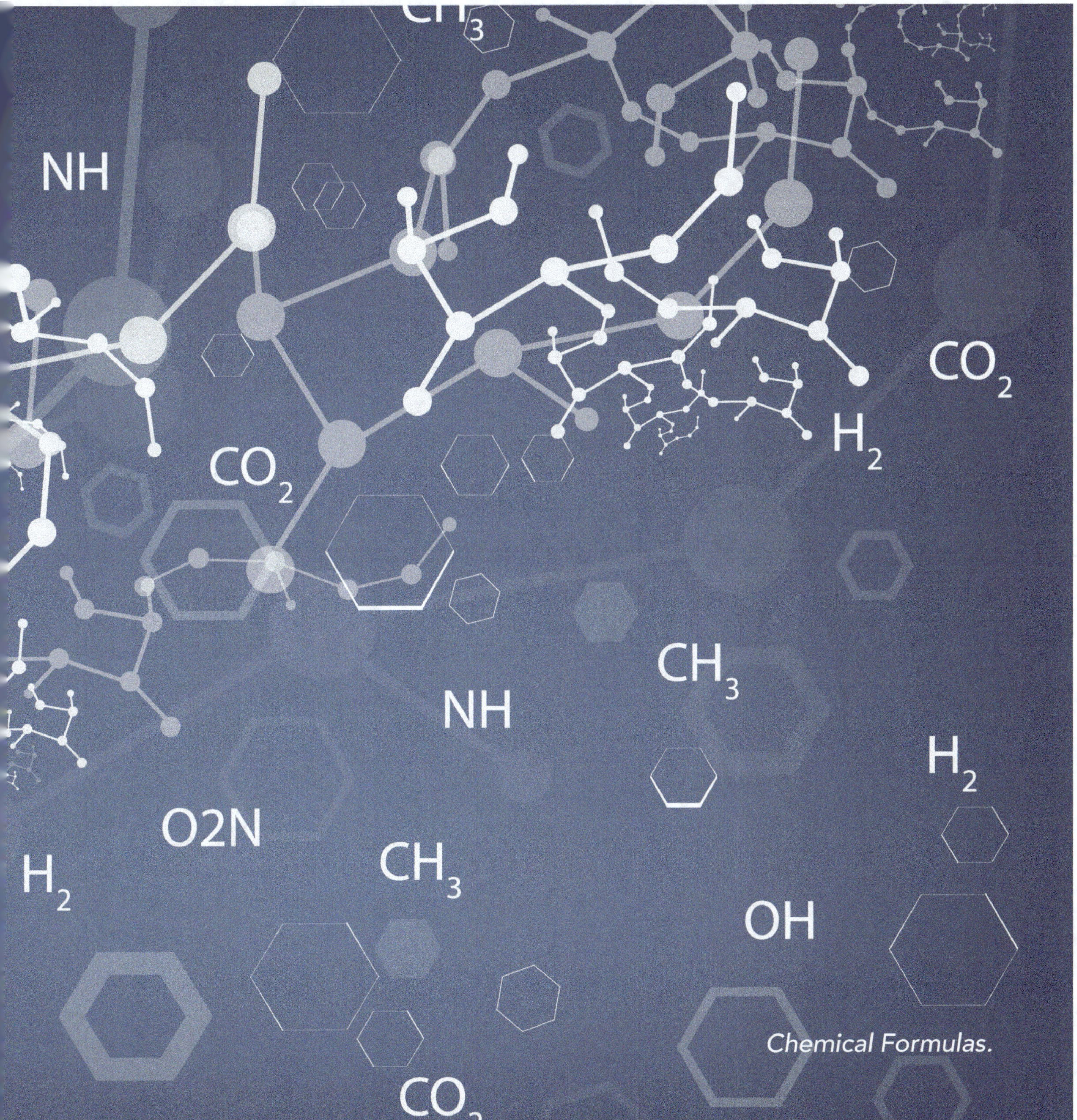

NH
CO₂
CH₃
CO₂
H₂
NH
CH₃
H₂
O2N
CH₃
OH
H₂
CO₂
Chemical Formulas.

WHAT IS A COMPOUND?

A chemical compound is made up of atoms of different elements joined together by a chemical bond. The bonds are so strong that the compound acts as if it were a single substance. The joined atoms form molecules, and the molecules connect together to make the compound.

Scientists list the elements in the Periodic Table of the Elements. The table gives important information about each element and its relation to the other elements near it.

Chemical compounds are made up of elements, but compounds can have different properties from the elements that make them up.

WHY NAME COMPOUNDS?

We give names to compounds because there are so many of them! When scientists are working, they want to make sure they are using the right compound, not one that is similar to it, but is different in some essential way. Think of the confusion if two scientists gave the same name to two different compounds and then tried to agree about what that compound was good for!

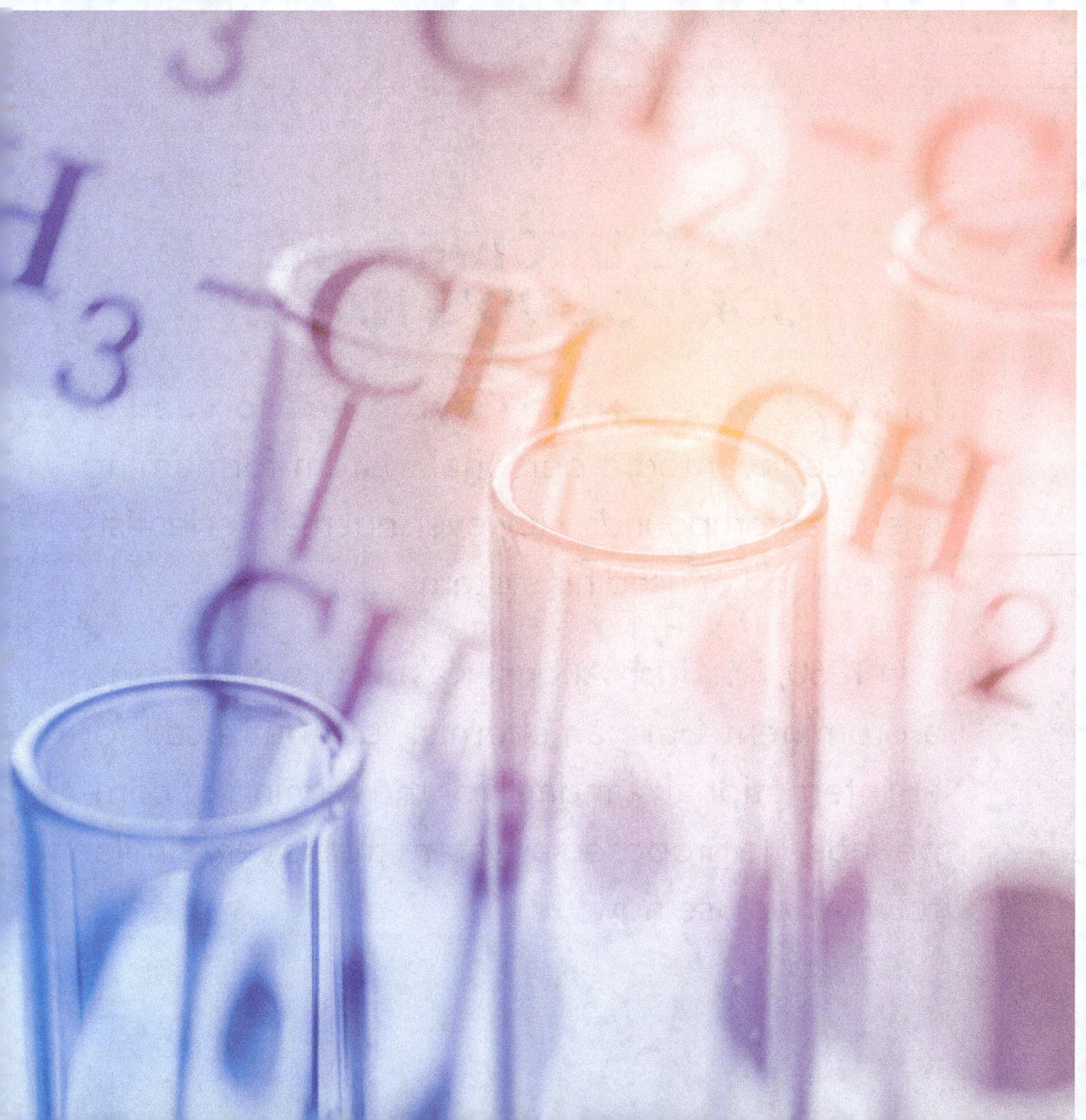

WHO DECIDES THE COMPOUND'S NAME?

In 1782, **Louis-Bernard Guyton de Morveau** of France invented a personal system for naming chemical compounds. However, not many scientists understood or used his system.

In 1860, **Friedrich August Kekulé von Stradonitz,** a prominent German chemist, put out a call for an international standard for the naming of compounds. He proposed a system that is very similar to what we use now.

In 1919, scientists founded the **International Union of Pure and Applied Chemistry,** or **IUPAC**. This organization took on responsibility for making a solid naming convention that all scientists could follow.

IUPAC has its headquarters in Switzerland and is accepted as the authority in this matter and others by scientists around the world.

TWO TYPES OF COMPOUNDS

There are basically two types of compounds. Which type the compound is depends on how its atoms bind together.

Molecular Compounds have molecules whose atoms bind to each other through *"Covalent"* bonds. In covalent bonds, the atoms share electrons and this sticks them together.

In **Ionic Compounds** or **Salts**, the atoms draw together because of the attraction between their positive and negative charges (or ions). Salts form what are called *"Crystalline Solids"*.

Salt crystals under the microscope.

THE RULES OF NAMING COMPOUNDS

You can name your cat or dog Spot or Tiger, or whatever you like. However, if you are naming a chemical you need to follow IUPAC's rules. This is very helpful when scientists in different laboratories, perhaps in different countries, want to work together to solve a problem or research something: they all know what they are supposed to be working with!

The naming process is not random. Each name describes the features of the compound: its atomic weight, its properties, and whether the compound is inorganic or organic.

Ni
Nickel
58.693
2-8-16-2
+3 45
Rh
Rhodium
102.91
2-8-18-16-1
+3 46
+2
+4
Pd
Palladium
106.42
2-8-18-18
77 +3
+4
Ir
Iridium
192.22
18-32-15-2
79
Au
Gold
196.97

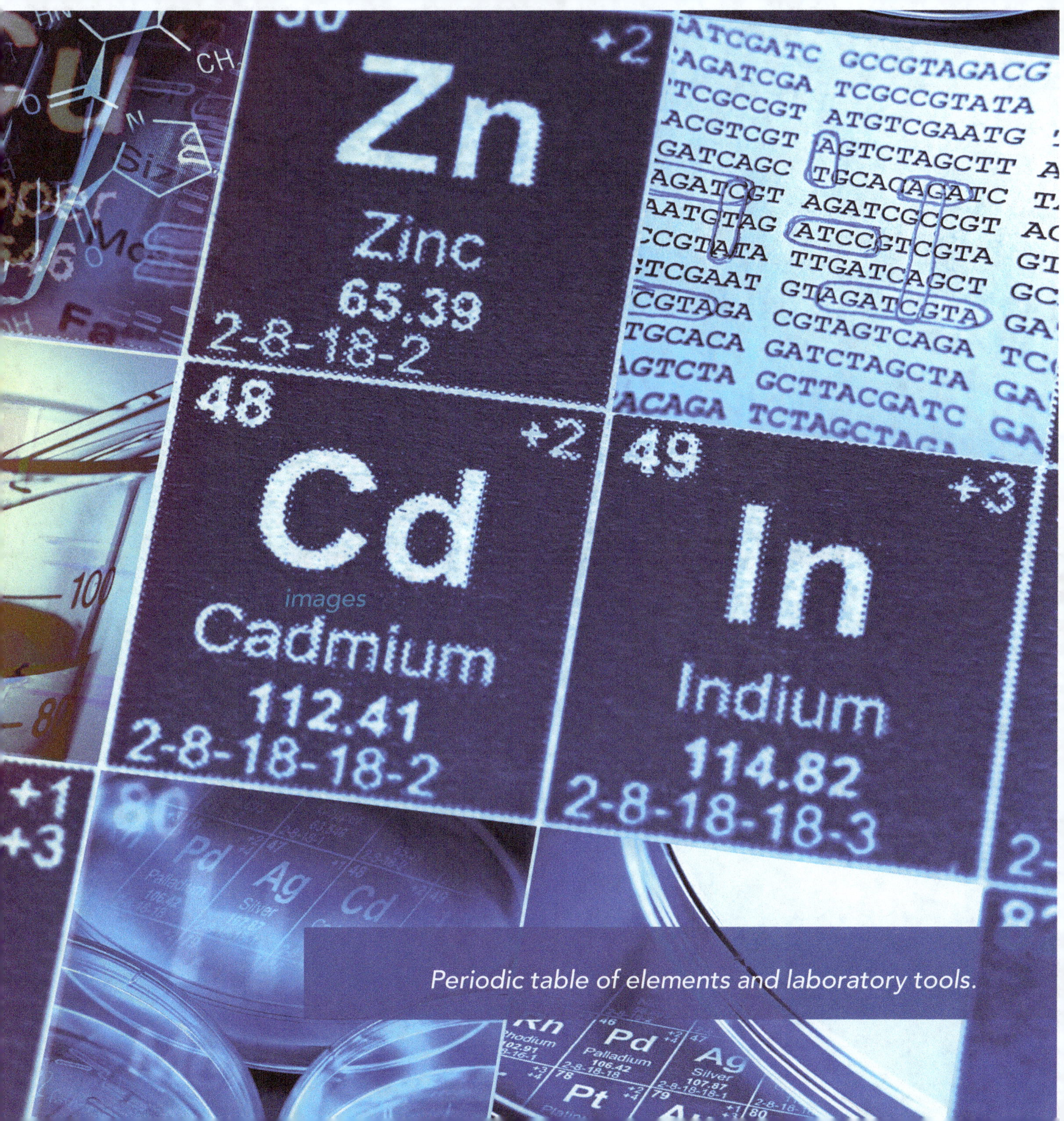

Periodic table of elements and laboratory tools.

NAMING AN IONIC COMPOUND

Ionic compounds contain a non-metal and a metal, so you can look on the Periodic Table of the Elements to see if the elements in this compound match the requirement.

Then you build the name: The first part of the name is the name of the metal in the compound. The second part of the name is based on the name of the non-metal element, plus the ending, or suffix, *"-ide"*.

For example, if you combine two atoms of aluminum (Al_2) with three atoms of oxygen (O_3), you get this compound: Al_2O_3. Instead of calling it "Al little 2 oh little 3", which could sound sort of silly and would not translate well into other languages, we take the name of the metal, add part of the name of the non-metal, and add the suffix "*-ide*" to get "*Aluminum Oxide*".

COMPOUNDS WITH TRANSITION METALS

Certain elements are called *"Transition Metals"* because they can have more than one charge and make more than one compound. When you write their names, you have to add a Roman numeral (I, II, III) to give more information about the compound.

Compounds with transition metals include $FeCl_2$ and $FeCl_3$, where Fe is Iron and Cl is Chlorine. The names of these compounds would be *"Iron (II) Chloride"* and *"Iron (III) Chloride"*.

Iron(III) chloride hexahydrate sample.

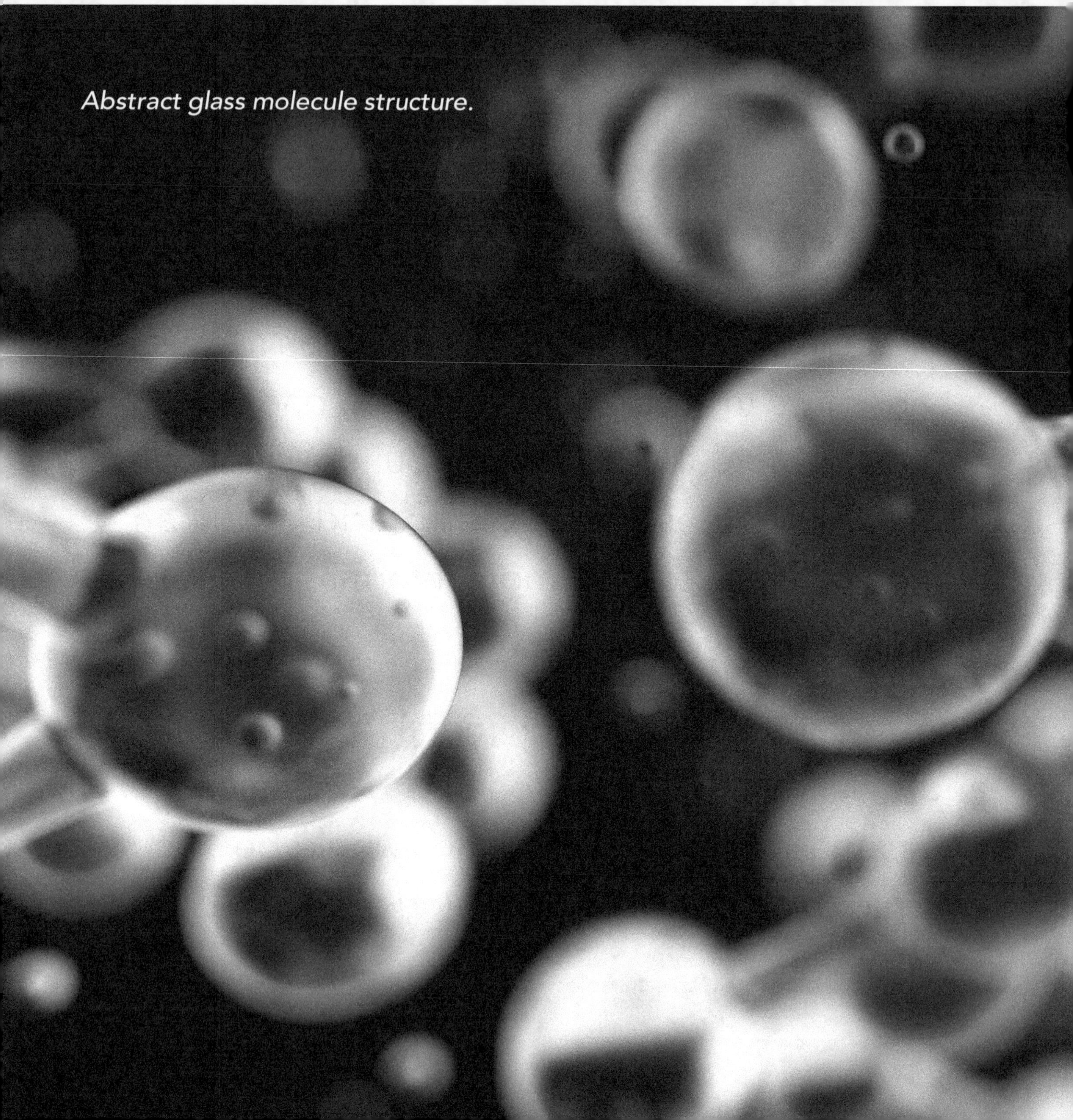
Abstract glass molecule structure.

NAMING COVALENT COMPOUNDS

Covalent compounds have atoms of two or more nonmetal elements. You build the name of the compound based on the number of each type of atom.

The prefixes that describe the numbers of atoms come from Latin. If you are going to work in a chemistry lab, you need to know the first ten prefixes without having to look them up. They are:

Mono - means 1 atom

Di - means 2 atoms

Tri - means 3 atoms

Tetra - means 4 atoms

Penta - means 5 atoms

Hexa - means 6 atoms

Hepta - means 7 atoms

Octa - means 8 atoms

Nona - means 9 atoms

and **Deca** - means 10 atoms

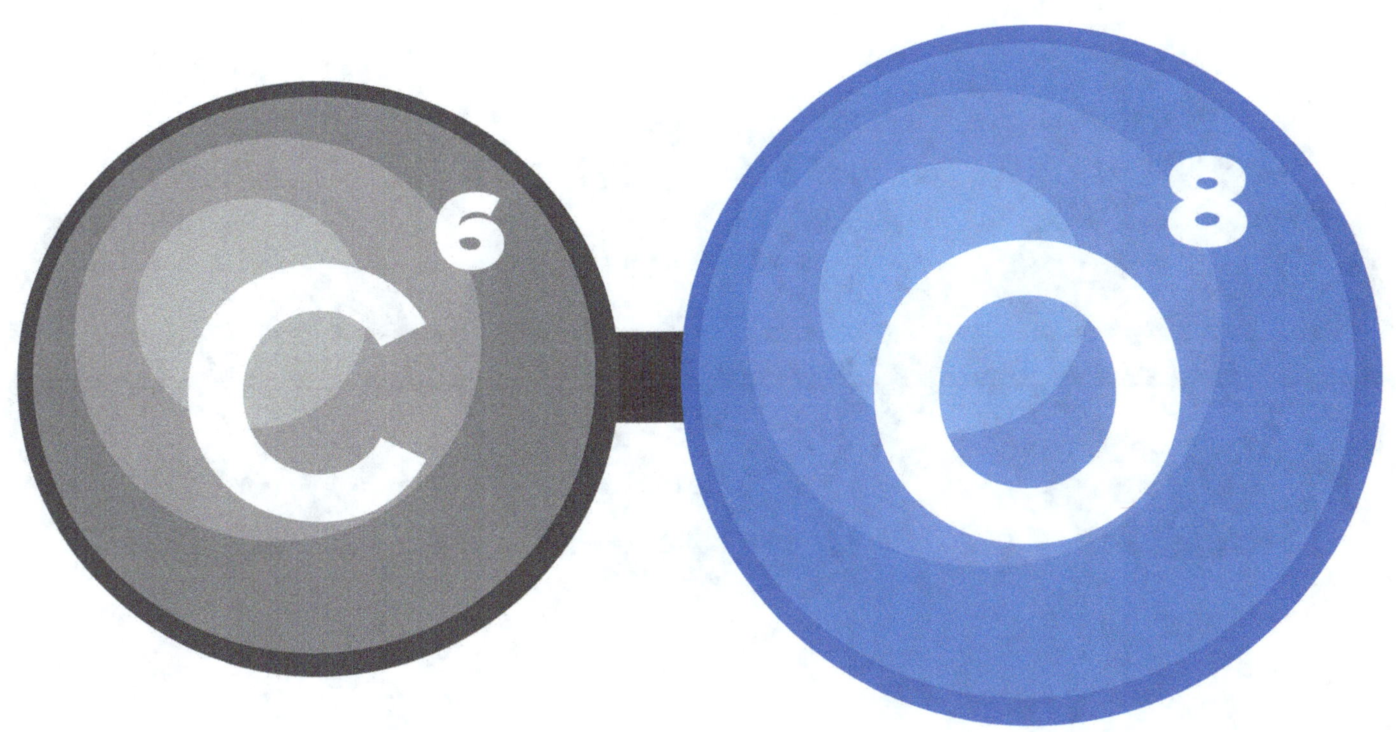

Carbon monoxide

Carbon dioxide

Here are some examples of how we use the element names and the prefixes for the names of covalent compounds:

C is Carbon and O is Oxygen. CO is *"Carbon Monoxide"*. CO_2 is *"Carbon Dioxide"*.

N is Nitrogen and S is Sulfa. N_2S_3 is *"Dinitrogen Trisulfide"*.

If there is just one atom of a particular element we don't have to use *"mono-"*. We keep on using it for *"Carbon Monoxide"* because this was one of the first compound names chemists established. It is just a habit, one that breaks the rule we just learned!

There are other exceptions to the rules. By tradition, we call $CaCl_2$ *"Calcium Chloride"*, not *"Calcium Dichloride"*.

Calcium chloride ($CaCl_2$) flakes.

NAMING POLYATOMIC COMPOUNDS

Polyatomic compounds have groups of atoms that bond together, and each group has a positive or a negative charge.

The names of polyatomic compounds have a different suffix. Most of them end with *"-ate"* or *"-ite"*. There are a few that end with *"-ide"*, like Cyanide, Hydroxide, and Peroxide.

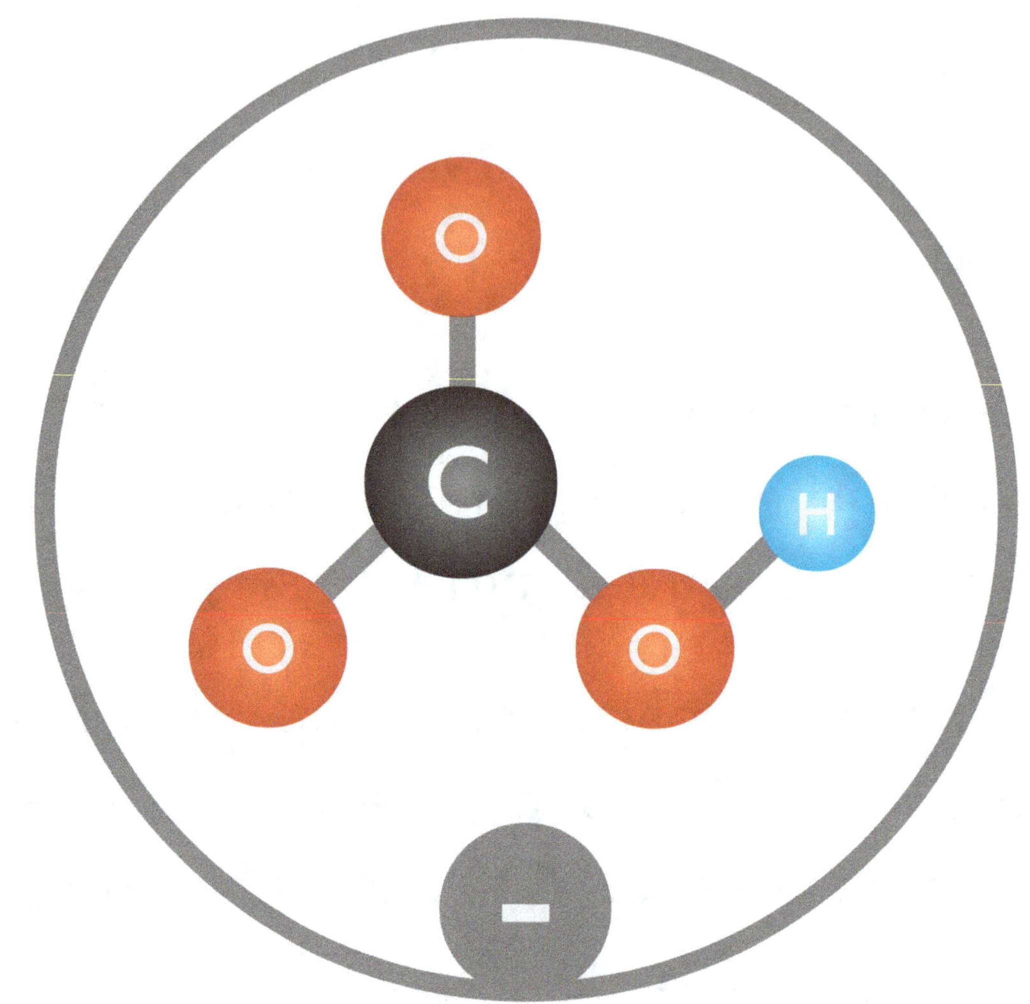

HCO₃⁻

Hydrogen Carbonate

Here are some naming examples:

H is Hydrogen, C is Carbon, and O is Oxygen, so CO_3 would be *"Carbonate"* and HCO_3 would be *"Hydrogen Carbonate"*.

Sometimes removing an atom changes the ending of the name. NO_3 is the inorganic compound *"Nitrate"*. NO_2 is *"Nitrite"* or *"Nitrogen Dioxide"*.

If you change the central atom to another atom from the same group on the Periodic Table of the Elements, the name changes: S is Sodium, O is Oxygen, and Se is Selenium; so SO_4 is *"Sulfate"* and SeO_4 is *"Selenate"*.

Intense pink of potassium permanganate solution turns purple when poured into sucrose and sodium hydroxide in water.

COMMON ION GROUPS

Here are the ion groups that form the basis of most polyatomic compounds.

OH is a *Hydroxide* ion

NO_3 is a *Nitrate* ion

HCO_3 is a *Hydrogen Carbonate* ion

MnO_4 is a *Permanganate* ion

CO_3 is a *Carbonate* ion

CrO_4 is a *Chromate* ion

Cr_2O_7 is a *Dichromate* ion

SO_4 is a *Sulfate* ion

SO_3 is a *Sulfite* ion

S_2O_3 is a *Thiosulfate* ion

PO_4 is a *Phosphate* ion

NH_4 is an *Ammonium* ion

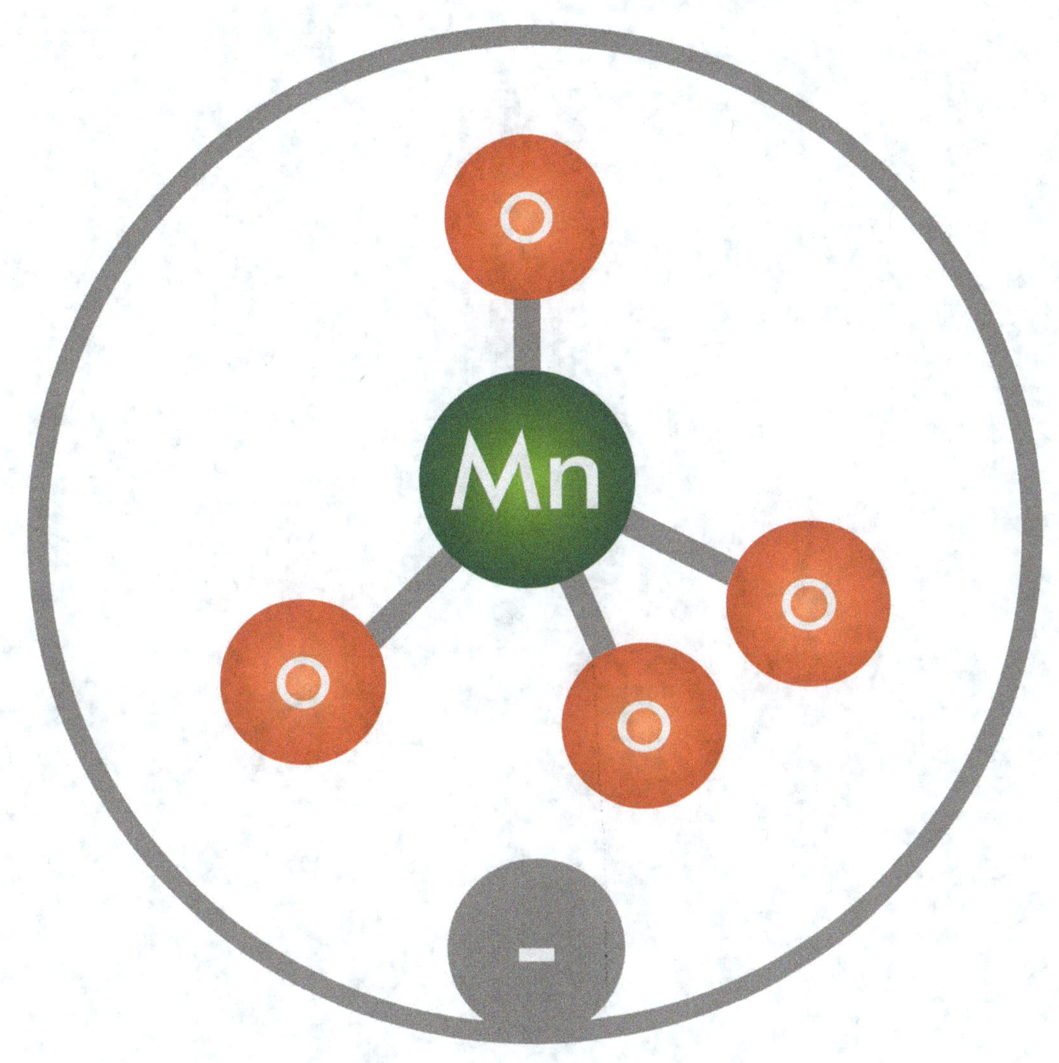

MnO$_4^-$

Permanganate

CATION (Positive Ions)

Potassium	K^+	Ammonium	NH_4^+	Tin (I	
Sodium	Na^+	Calcium	Ca^{2+}	Lead	
Lithium	Li^+	Magnesium	Mg^{2+}	Copp	
Hydrogen	H^+	Zinc	Zn^{2+}	Mang	
Argentums (I)	Ag^+	Barium	Ba^{2+}	Alum	
Mercury (I)	Hg^+			Iron (	
				Iron (	
				Chror	

ANION (Negative Ions)

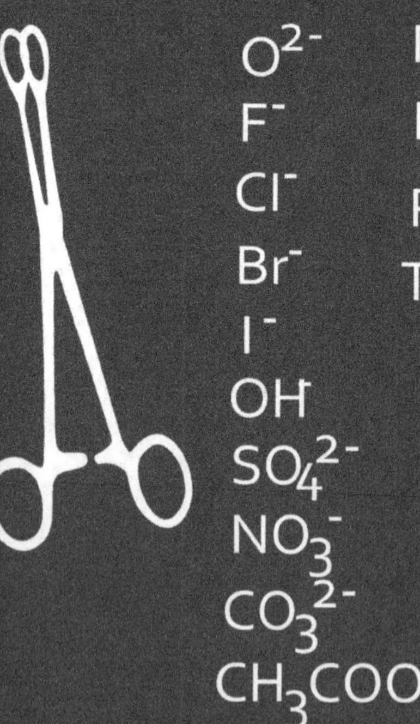

Oxide	O^{2-}	Manganate	MnO_4^-
Fluoride	F^-	Dichromate	$Cr_2O_7^{2-}$
Chloride	Cl^-	Phosphate	PO_4^{3-}
Bromide	Br^-	Thiosulphate	$S_2O_3^{2-}$
Iodide	I^-		
Hydroxide	OH^-		
Sulphate	SO_4^{2-}		
Nitrate	NO_3^-		
Carbonate	CO_3^{2-}		
Ethanoate	CH_3COO^-		

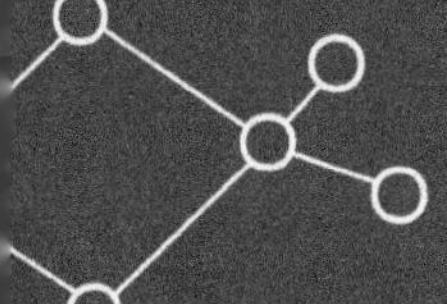

FORMULA FOR CERTAIN MOLECULE

Sn^{2+}	Carbon Monoxide	CO
Pb^{2+}	Carbon Dioxide	CO_2
Cu^{2+}	Nitrogen Monoxide	NO
Mn^{2+}	Nitrogen Dioxide	NO_2
Al^{3+}	Sulphur Dioxide	SO_2
Fe^{2+}	Sulphur Trioxide	SO_3
Fe^{3+}	Fluorine	F_2
Cr^{3+}	Bromine	Br_2
	Chlorine	Cl_2
	Iodine	I_2
	Ammonia	NH
	Water	H_2O
	Hydrogen Chloride	$HC1$
	Tetrachloromethane	$CC1_4$
	Glucose	$C_6H_{12}O_6$
	Hydrogen Bromide	HBr
	Hydrogen Iodide	HI
	Hydrogen Sulphide	H_2S
	Ethanol	C_2H_5OH
	Ethanoic Acid	CH_3COOH

II)

I)

THE ORDER OF
THE NAMES

With binary compounds, molecules with two elements, the name of the compound has two words, starting with the name of the element at the left in the formula. Part of the name of the second element gets combined with *"ide"*, like this:

O is Oxygen, so where it is the second element in the formula the word we use is *"Oxide"*.

Cl is Chlorine, which becomes *"Chloride"*.

Br is Bromine, which becomes *"Bromide"*.

F is Fluorine, which becomes *"Fluoride"*.

NaCl
SODIUM CHLORIDE

Here are some compound names:

Na is Sodium and Cl is Chlorine. NaCl is *"Sodium Chloride"*.

Mg is Magnesium and S is Sulfur. MgS is *"Magnesium Sulfide"*.

If the compound has a metal element and a non-metal element, the name of the metal element comes first. So a compound containing Iron and Fluoride, the compound name would start with *"Iron"*.

If there are two non-metal elements, the first name of the compound is the name of the element that is on the left in the Periodic Table of the Elements. For example, for a compound containing carbon and oxygen, the name would start with *"carbon"* because carbon is further to the left on the Periodic Table.

Sodium chloride

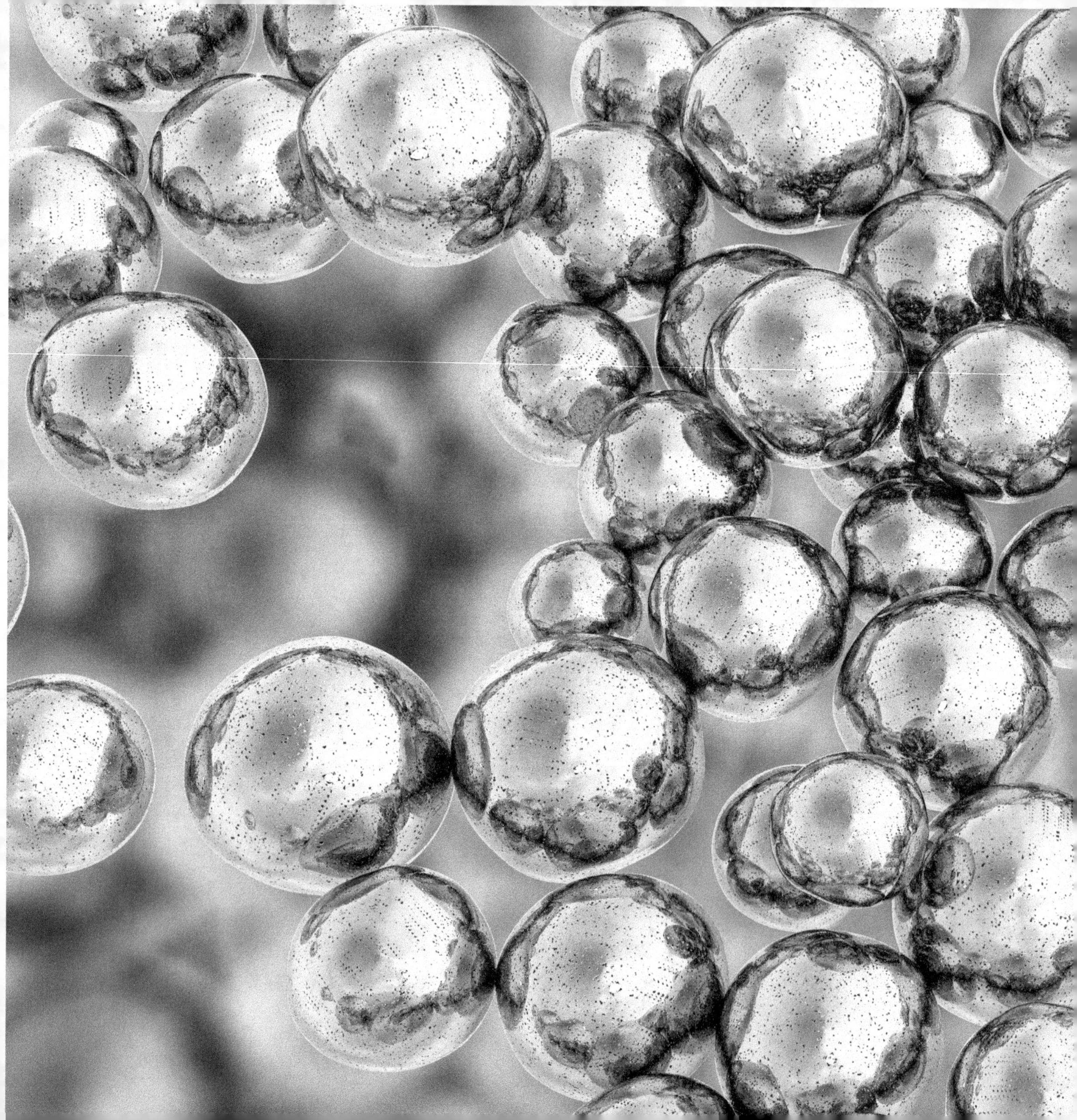

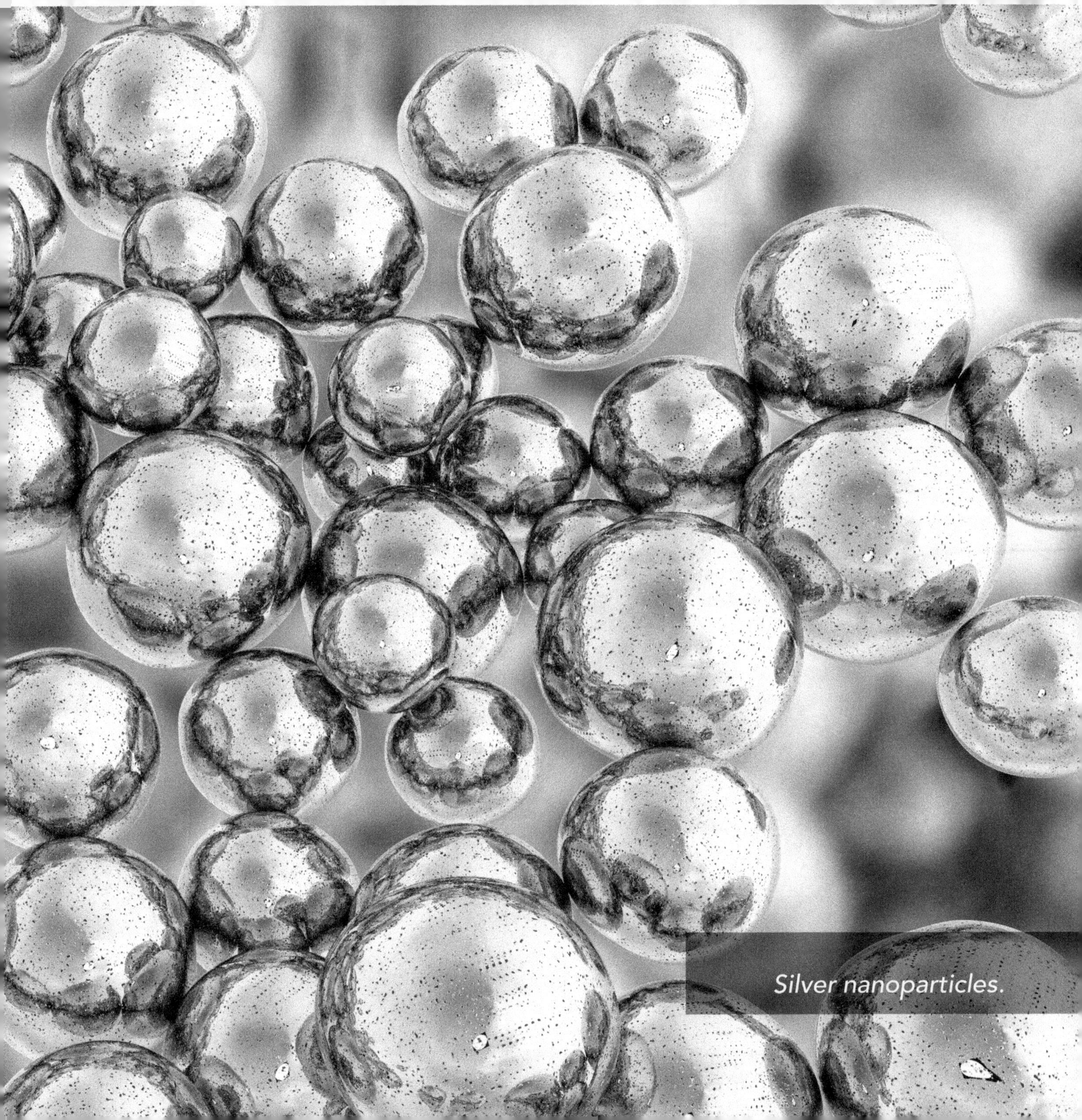

Silver nanoparticles.

MORE COMPLEX RULES

t doesn't stop here, because the world is complicated!

Naming metal-non-metal compounds

If one of the two elements in a compound is a metal, as we mentioned before, you use a Roman numeral to indicate which ion uses the charge. For example, **Ag** is Silver and **C** is Chlorine. **Ag_2Cl_2** is *"Silver (II) Dichloride"*.

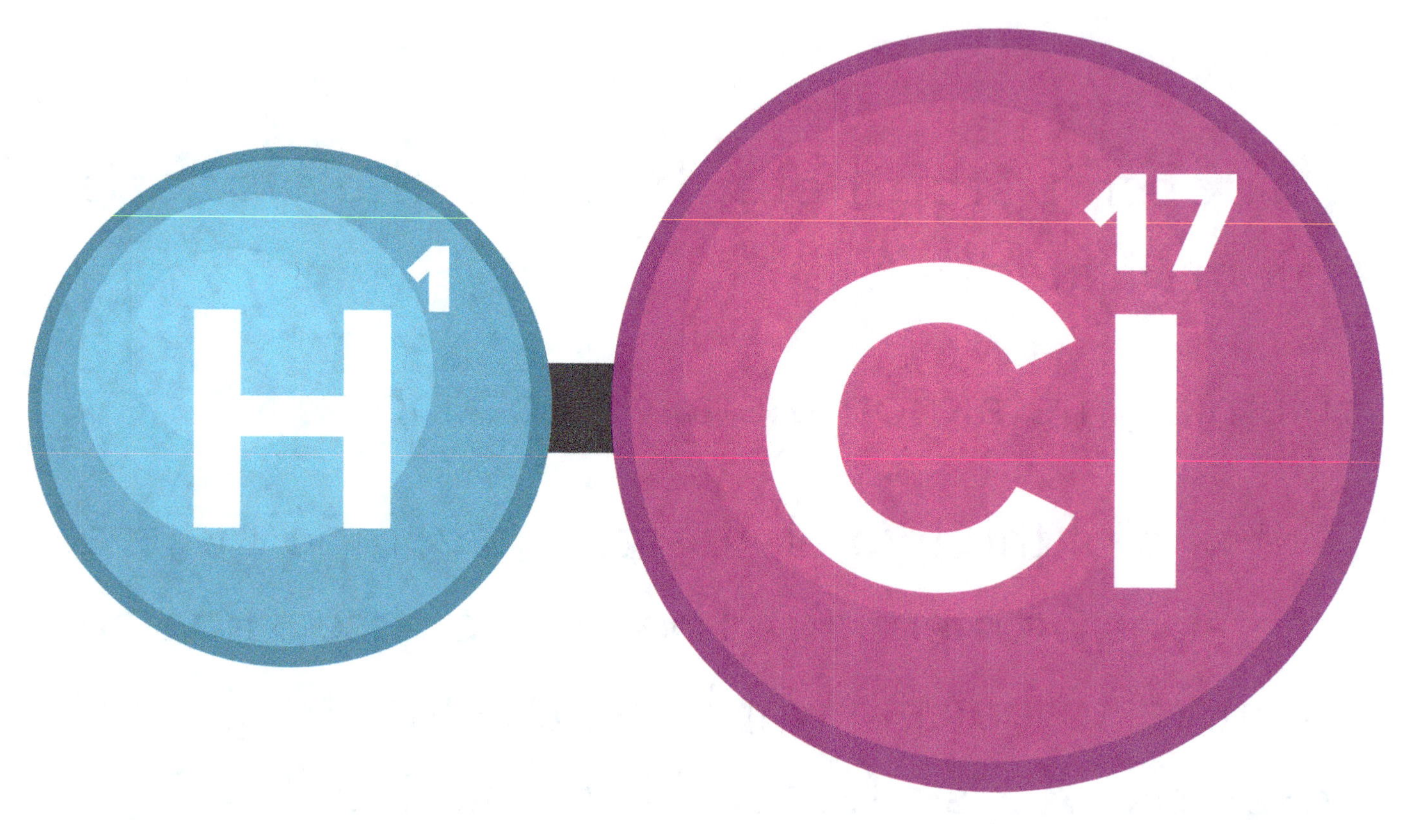

Hydrochloric acid

NAMING ACIDS

For hydro acids chemists start the name with *"hydro-"* and add *"-ic"* at the end of the name. For example, **H** is Hydrogen and **F** is Fluorine. **HF** is *"Hydrofluoric Acid"*. Since **Cl** is Chlorine, **HCl** would be *"Hydrochloric Acid"*.

For some acids, the *"-ic"* goes at the end of the name of the element that is bonded to the most oxygen atoms. H_2SO_4 is *"Sulfuric Acid"*, and HNO_3 is *"Nitric Acid"*.

LEARN ABOUT THIS WONDERFUL EARTH

Chemistry, Physics, Biology, and Geology help us understand ourselves and the world we live in. Read other Baby Professor books, like *What is Organic Chemistry?*, *The Things Chemists Use in Chemical Labs,* and *How Noble are Noble Gases?* to learn even more!

Visit
BABY PROFESSOR
EDUCATION KIDS
www.BabyProfessorBooks.com
to download Free Baby Professor eBooks
and view our catalog of new and exciting
Children's Books

www.ingramcontent.com/pod-product-compliance
Lightning Source LLC
Chambersburg PA
CBHW060139120726
48003CB00009B/2948